# FRIENDLY
## CALIFORNIA GRAY WHALES

by Sanjay Patel

PEARSON

Glenview, Illinois • Boston, Massachusetts • Chandler, Arizona
Upper Saddle River, New Jersey

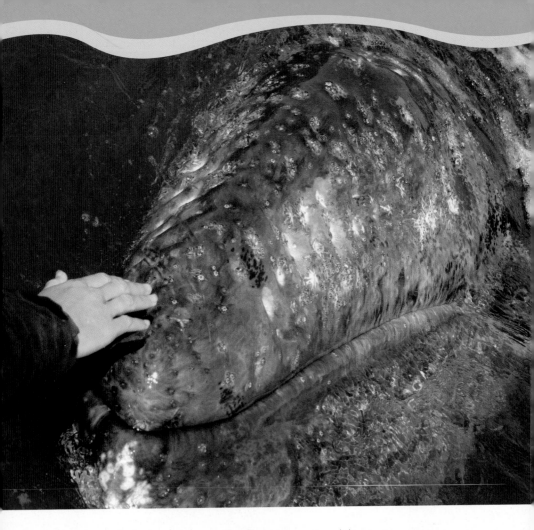

Each year, gray whales migrate. Migrate means "move far away." Gray whales start out in Alaska. They swim way down to Mexico. They go to a lagoon there called *Laguna San Ignacio*.

They have their babies in the warm water. Whale babies are called calves.

Laguna San Ignacio is a special place. Whales swim up to boats. People can touch them!

The first time this happened was in 1976. Friendly whales came close to a fisherman's boat. He petted the whale and her calf.

Nobody knows why the whales come close to boats.

## FACTS ABOUT CALIFORNIA GRAY WHALES

**Number:** There are about 26,000 gray whales.

**Size:** They can be 50 feet long. They can weigh 80,000 pounds. New babies weigh 1,500 pounds!

**Feeding:** Whales eat tiny animals. The whales suck sand into their mouths. Then they push the sand through the baleen. A whale's baleen is like a comb. Tiny animals in the sand get trapped in the baleen. The sand falls out.

## GRAY WHALE

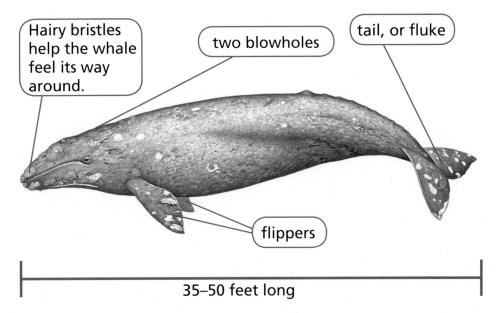

Hairy bristles help the whale feel its way around.

two blowholes

tail, or fluke

flippers

35–50 feet long

The gray whale is long and thin. Its shape helps it swim fast.

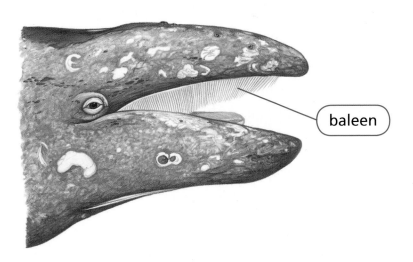

baleen

A gray whale does not have teeth. It has baleen instead. Baleen traps the whale's food.

Salty water helps calves float.

**Calves:** Mother whales have one calf every two years. The calves nurse for seven months. They drink 50 gallons of milk each day! This helps them make blubber. Blubber is thick fat that keeps whales warm.

Calves stay with their mothers for three months. Their mothers teach them to swim.

**Migrating:** Gray whales migrate far each year. In the summer, they stay near Alaska. In the fall, they swim south. They stay near Mexico for the winter. In the spring, they go back north. Each trip takes two or three months. Whales travel 14,000 miles round trip!

Migration route of the California gray whale

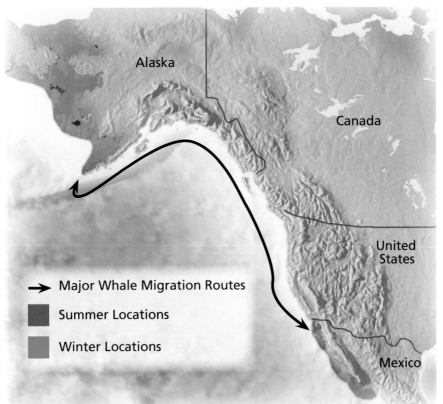

Alaska

Canada

United States

Mexico

→ Major Whale Migration Routes

Summer Locations

Winter Locations

Why do gray whales migrate so far? Maybe it's because the lagoon is just right for them. The lagoon is not deep. The water is warm and salty. Salt water helps the calves float. Animals that eat calves do not live in the lagoon. It is a safe place.

Many people like to pet the gray whales. Would you?

## Extend Language — Whale Migration Words

These words tell about whale migration:

| Adjectives | Nouns | Verbs |
| --- | --- | --- |
| • long | • trip | • stay |
| • warm | • Pacific Ocean | • spend |
| • cold | • lagoon | • swim |
| | | • migrate |